Life in a Body

By Isla M. Grimhilde

Dedicated To Rose
I miss you

What's This All About

Part memories, part diary, and just thinking out loud, this is a record of my journey to be a healthier person. To get there I need to go to the past, look at what I'm doing right now, and try to figure out where I'm going, not to mention, where I want to be. So much thinking about food and emotions. So much to untangle and put together again.

My body sucks and I am ot fond of living in it. However there are no other options. So if I'm going to be happy I need to make peace with that and all that goes along with that. There have been many mistakes and so much wasted time. Dear reader please learn from all the dumb mistakes and idoit thoughts I've had. Peace and truth are so much better than self-loathing and chasing a number. If I seem to go back and forth that's because I am.

Maybe when I'm done I'll have a more authentic voice, better health, and be thin. Or not, I don't know. I guess if I'm just making progress then that will be enough. Progress on this journey is what I'm here for.

So tired of my poor coping skills, tired of stress, and just not being able to enjoy myself. These bad skills are holding me back. All the things that I really want from life happen so much easier without my food rules and misuse. It's time for me to be in charge of my mind. Really in charge.

Most of my life is going back and forth, so here is my mind's process laid out before the world.

The process I am using this time around is Intuitive Eating, a little CBT, and some ACT. I've got an app called Calm. Those tools and writing my feelings is what I'm doing to get past my over eating. No diets this time around. God help me get through this.

Looking for the Lost Voice

Well there once was a time I could write with my heart and pepper my soul in through my words. Like a mystical fabric of truth, my voice would snige the paper with truth. So beautiful, so raw, so full of life. Then there was change. Things that robbed me of my voice, left the truth for control, and the honesty that was both shocking and fresh became dulled and bleached by my need to be tame, not wild. So here I am, old, full of things that are being held back, and trying to break the dam. I'm not ready for this, I'm watered down.

There is no greatness in me. At one time I thought there was, that I had a spark of something special. Nothing is new or that special, I am but a reflection of the beauty that is God. It's amazing and special, but so ordinary it's painful. This is what we all are.

I'm fat. In between words I'm having cheese with onions. That is who I am right now. Someone who stuffs down her emotions with food. A thousand starts but never following through. An endless list of excuses to not do the things I should. I'm dyslexic, I'm a mess, I have OCD, I'm too old, I'm too fat, I'm too dumb, I'm not dumb enough, I'm noty pretty enough, I'm too disconnected, I'm too tired. I was not meant to be successful. My time has passed me by.

There is hope inside me.

My direction is the way the wind takes me. Too tired of this, but too comfortable to make a change. Comfort makes me flabby in my body and mind. The cheese is gone, the soda remains. It's comfortable to watch TV. Life has become watching more than doing.

I don't want to be fat. That's a preoccupation that takes my mind and numbs all the real problems I have. It's a distraction, and to keep it up I must sabotage my own health. I wreck my own touch with truth and lose my observations. Pain is too rough.

I really don't know how to feel. Being in a body seems like I'm far away playing with strings of a puppet or using an avatar. Not sure where my consciousness is, but I know it's beyond my body, in another layer or something, like a quantum field of the soul.

Emotions live in my flesh. Being far from them is safe, but I don't feel really alive anymore.

I'm eating all the time. Sugar is my drug. No other food has me hooked, I eat sugar and it softly puts me to sleep. The next day I feel awful. If it has so much energy why do I feel so sleepy after I eat it?

I don't know if I can feel anything. My body and soul are not as close as they should be. This is the ghost life in a body. I can't even sing anymore.

Things often don't turn out the way we play them.

Can remember a day many years ago when my grandfather decided my brother and I should see snow. What reason he had for this I will never know, but he took my grandma, my little brother and me in a mustang and headed in land. The ride took a few hours and it was slow going. Trucks were everywhere. The weather was miserable. The cold was of a sort I had never experienced before. Finally, my grandmother had enough and made my grandpa pull over when we were going into the mountains and make a little snowman.

Snow wasn't what I thought it would be like. This was the wet kind. Instead of soft cotton like fabric, it was a slushy with no flavor. My grandma made a little snowman and put him in the freezer. The look on my grandpa's face told me this was not a proper snowman. This was a snowman of shame. A quitter's snowman. We turned around and once we got home the snowman was put in the freezer. There he lived for many months. The day my mother took him out and let him melt in the sun I cried. Is it a tragedy that we didn't go all the way to Tahoe and build a tower of a snowman while we engaged in epic snowball fights? The memory of that day is still with me. Nothing sticks out more than the air making the metal of the car so cold. It was a day I will never forget.

8

Sometimes I think my voice is like Peter Pan's shadow. It has a life of its own. What I really need is for it to be sewn back on. By the time I'm done writing this I hope I can feel again and be in touch with my truth.

Food

Why is food my armor? Big gooey safety blanket that protects from nothing. Not having enough of it and then having way too much caused me so much pain. Then there's soda. What I wouldn't do for it. I cried for soda when I was still in the crib.

Soda is the perfect drug. Loaded with caffeine and sugar it gives me that one-two punch of energy and mellowness. Probably if I ever tried cocaine I'd be in trouble.

It took me a long time to circle back to addiction. Most food isn't that much of a draw for me. I hate eating. It causes me anxiety. So much angst over if I'm eating a good or a bad food and if I'm taking too much. The siren call of sugar is nothing compared to caffeine. Even now I still can't stop consuming it.

It has been a long time, several years, since I've binged on food. Still I wonder if my overeating of sugar isn't a binge? Perhaps it is. Once, many years ago, I went to Overeaters Anonymous. The food addiction didn't really fit with me. Getting treatment for my eating disorder helped me so much. Perhaps there is a little addiction to that sugar going on.

The best way for me to eat is fasting combined with all meat. This is very expensive, but it takes away cravings. It also makes my skin glow, and has made my bones strong. I don't think this is a diet for everyone, but it really works for me. Still, I don't find it easy to pay for good meat so I tend to stray.

Life is taking and giving. We take in water, and then expel it. Air comes in the body and we cleave it in two and breathe out what the trees need. They do the same back. Food is something that was once alive, we need to devour it and give back what the earth needs to make things grow. The sun creates this energy. Once this dance ends we die. Giving all the body back to the soil.

Food is the earth my mother is buried beneath. It's also the barrier between me and my feelings. If someone ever says that feelings aren't dangerous, they haven't felt mine.

I'm getting help but my eating is getting worse. Maybe it's a darkest before the dawn thing, or I need something else.

Food becomes hard to resist at night and when I'm angry. Perhaps eating is an act of defiance for me. A way of standing up to the beast. After all, she never wanted me to eat. When I was five a friend's mother asked her if she thought of putting me on a diet. The beast admitted that I had been on one for a long time.

I don"t know what to eat. The thought of eating seems fun. The act of eating is not, not fun at all. Medication is keeping me from compulsively eating and eating at night. It's so strange. My anxiety is sort of manageable I suppose. But the thought of food is so much. For some reason I am the one who goes shopping and prepares the food for the family. It is bizarre that it has fallen on me. I guess it's because it's a mom job. Not a great choice for me, probably about as bad as it can get. At least I don't work in a restaurant.

I'm eating during the day. Slowly I find that I am not getting as anxious when I eat. Last night I had some apples and I enjoyed them. As I ate them I did not think about what I would eat next or have racing thoughts. I just ate them and let it go. It was strange but very natural. Finding normal things as strange is sobering. It shouldn't be that hard to just eat. I have enough, I can eat what I want, when I want, and as much as I like.

So here I am. Been a little while and I'm eating less at night. It shouldn't be this hard but I really don't know what to do or how to eat. A person of my age should not be so confused about food. I hate food and I wish I never had to think about it again. It's been a long day. Today I ate cereal. A whole bowl of the poison.

I have made a vow to eat only when I'm hungry. This might seem sort of obvious, but it is not so simple for me. There is so much going on in my head when I eat other than just hunger.

First I think if the food is a proper food or a fun food. A proper food is fine to eat, but not too much of it. Usually it is pretty but has no flavor. Fun foods sound like they should be just that, but are the opposite. Before I eat them I think about them, daydream, plan how to get them, get upset if I can't, but then when they are in front of me there is no fun. Only anxiety and thinking about what I will eat, not what I'm eating now. Then there is the shame and the unpleasant feeling afterwards.

Eating when I'm hungry is a tough idea, but what to eat is just unthinkable. Coming up with a healthy diet that isn't so black and white drives me crazy. And I really don't need any help with that. God made me that way.

Today I waited until I felt hungry to eat. It took until 3:30, and then I went to the store and I made good choices. All I bought was nuts, meat, and cheese. It took a long time to get home so I ate around 4:30. Slowing down and enjoying my food was really hard. As hard as I tried I could only muster up a little courage to savor my meat a little. When my mind would wander to what I was going to eat next I did my best to bring it back to what was in front of me instead. The nuts were not so great. The meat was awesome. The cheese was ok. The feeling after I ate was fantastic. Truly I ate a lot, but I didn't over eat.

I saw pastries when I was at the store. Cakes and cookies were there as well, and I was hungry. Very hungry. The feeling hit me after I had finished with work and I drove to the store. It's not the best idea to shop in such a state. To be safe I did not go down the aisles and was only tempted in the bakery. Made it home and ate. Meat makes me poop though. And poop and poop.

Today I again waited to eat until I was hungry. The feeling came around eleven am and I ate leftover roast. There are so many things going on. Terrible things to worry about. Yet here I am, worried about food again. Thinking about and wondering if I ate too much, did I eat enough, did I eat the right thing, when will I have to eat next, and all those other thoughts that fill my mind. It takes my mind off of all those other hard to think about things.

This is not a new thought. I've been pushing away difficult thoughts with worries about food for so long I can't remember when I started. After all, what is more vital than eating? Only water and air matter more.

There is something buried deep in my DNA that needs to think about getting the next meal. Past generations didn't eat as well as we do today. It's an easy and natural thing to worry about. No food is death. If I could save the world from starvation, I would.

The house smells of food. This makes me happy. It's strange that the smell of cooking food makes me feel so homey and safe. Eating it causes so much distress. It's getting better, but the thought of eating isn't pleasant.

This was a success as far as eating goes. But as far as other things go I can't say so. There are many things I really need to work on. Right now I'm not certain how I want my diet to go. Such a distraction from everything. Maybe I should address my problems. If only I didn't have any of those. Then I wouldn't have to create problems with food that aren't as unpleasant. So tiresome.

Food is sacred. It connects us to this earth. All of nature must eat. Getting food is the main occupation of each and every living creature. Being respectful of food is not just good for the body, it's good for the soul.

I hate food.

Needing it, taking energy is so tiresome. I just wish I could get by on the air that I breathe.

Food and I need to lay down arms and rest. As gross as it is, and unseemingly messy, it is life. That which resides deep inside me must have this exchange. Food is the only way to keep life in a body.

Today food tasted good. It was not the best food I've ever had, but I liked it. Food isn't my enemy. It's just food.

That Group That Watches Weight

This is a tough topic for me. I both love and hate this organization. Long ago I went lifetime. Never will I go back. Not only have I rejected them I have also outgrown them. It's a weak way to fix a complex problem.

Back when I was 16 my doctor sent me there. Not much else was available for us obese people at the time. The group met in a church. Prayer was not a bad idea. Weighing in public was supposed to humiliate the body into submission. The body doesn't care.

Not that it was all bad. In fact it was the only hope I had. So I clung to it and made it work. Now I had been in a cycle since I was small of having food and then not having it. Giving my all to dieting when I was 16 changed this cycle into binging.

Those Thursday night meetings were full of older women who had very different problems from me. They were not typically as fat as I was. They had not been fat at my age. Most of them wanted to lose 30 pounds or so and were not very successful. My weight would go up and down. In general it was trending down and I made good progress. By the time a year had passed by I was down about 60 pounds.

The journey was full of hardship and self-denial. Not eating when you are hungry does strange things to your psyche. My eating problems were getting more ingrained. With each passing day I started to find myself thinking about food and eating more and more. Much of my day was spent planning meals, thinking about what a good weight would be, and how upset I was about what I ate.

Even though I had hit a good weight I wanted to get lower. I cut my calories and my weight loss slowed. I stopped eating much other than salad, but then I'd binge. Big binges where I couldn't stop eating. My weight crept down. Finally I got down to a place that wasn't horrible, I had lost 70 pounds. Now I was cured.

I promptly gained back 20 pounds.

Thus the cycle began.

I was not cured.

Even though the program wasn't working, I just blamed myself and kept at it. This was not when I went lifetime. That came years later. One thing about me, I am stubborn.

The real problem for me with this group was the first change. I was going along, believing that the diet was THE answer. If I did it, if I followed it, then I would lose weight. And they changed it. Part of the group was the benevolence of them changing the diet and how grateful we must be for all that the new diet allowed. I hated that. Were we being lied to before? Was the old diet crap? Was that why it wasn't working that well?

When I joined there was full choice, limited choice, and no choice. Which turned out was just horrible and had to be changed into exchanges. That, of course, turned out to be no good as well. Enter fat and fiber. Then came fat fobic calorie counting, the pointy kind. It isn't really that good either and needs to be constantly changed as well. You know why?

The diet isn't very good. The magic of the group is just the group. Weighing for shame isn't really important, just being in the group, being together, meeting once a week, preferably in a church, and sharing the pain, that's what helps.

Even though I know what a sham it is I thought about going back because there was a leader there I really liked. But when I checked she had gone. Outgrown them as well. Started her own group, her village. I guess she realized where the magic was too. Maybe I should do the same, but without the expensive price tag.

I could put an ad on Craig's List for some people who need support with life. Meet in the park on Thursday nights. Maybe one by a church. Talk about food and how we should respect it. Saying grace should replace eating with shame. No money to be made, just pure healing from a group of friends supporting each other. That might be nice.

Oh they have gone after children again. Why can't they just stop? If I was more inclined I'd lobby against such abuse of kids. Diets for children should be the work of doctors.

That Book That Says Health is More Important Than Size

This was a revelation for me. The thing about this philosophy that changed my life is the idea of putting health first. Not that I should just give up on weight management, but that I could, and should, do things that support my health. Losing weight is fine, as long as it doesn't sacrifice my well being and my health.

For so long my goal was just to be smaller. Losing weight became an obsession. Sometimes I was very, very good at it. Sometimes I was horrible at it. The idea of food being not full of shame was an amazing revelation. This book changed my life.

It is a very subtle change, but a big one. Health at Every Size did not stop me from tracking my food or walking to lose weight. But it did help me from doing this compulsively. I don't remember how many years ago I read that book. It was a great find.

Part of the book was not very helpful. It got kind of political. I am very well aware of how socially acceptable it is to pick on fat people. The book talked about this but called it thin privilege. I disagree that this exists. There are advantages to being thin. This is undeniable. People are rude to fat people for other reasons. It's fashionable.

When I was a young girl in kindergarten I was teased, and followed and harassed every day by some of the kids. They called me names. The favorites were Fatso and Fat Albert. They would do this until I was in tears. Every recess, every day. There was another girl they picked on as well, even more than me. She was tiny. It was hurtful and cruel.

Still, I am an internally driven person. The jabs about my height and my skin color never bothered me. It was that weight thing that really hurt. Being fat was something I just didn't want to be.I knew there was something wrong with it and I didn't like the way it looked. Fat limits movement and I knew that wasn't good. If I could move better I could have gotten away from those horrible people at school. Thank God we have evolved to the point that behavior like that gets schools sued these days.

I really don't believe in thin privilege. It's more like fat misery. When a person is unhappy and unhealthy it doesn't draw people in.

Getting healthy will make things better in every way. It's a very good book and philosophy, but don't give up on monitoring food choices all together. Just don't make losing weight a priority over health, physical or mental.

This was a really great concept, but these days it's more of a forget about size as a health marker philosophy. Of course there are those who are larger and are healthy, but it's not to be ignored completely. Especially by those of us who get to a size that becomes an issue because being that size is unhealthy in and of itself.

That Group For Those Who Are Addicted to Food

These folks are very genuine and nice. Always I just assumed that I must be addicted to food. It made a logical sort of sense. One day I decided to go to a meeting. They were very upfront with me. Many people don't understand what food addiction is. This was true for me.

I don't want to go into details about the meeting. Very moving and real, the people shared what it was to walk in their lives. They did not use food as I did at all. They used it for pleasure.

Truly I felt a kinship, a connection to those people, but I was different. Food was our master, but it ruled our lives in different ways. Very different ways.

After the meeting I read through the materials and joined some online groups. Reading through the 12 steps I found them to be foriegn. They didn't speak to me at all. This was not for me. God bless you if you do.

That Time I Thought That I'd Just Eat Clean

It looked so promising. Tosca Reno was so convincing, and I hope she is helping someone. That someone is not me. Eating clean is a joke. It's a terrible way for those of us who are diabetic to eat. Six meals a day might be great for some people. Body builders to be precise. This way of eating was designed by them to build muscle and gain weight. Why did I think I was going to lose weight doing this?

I drank a whole pitcher of that kool-aid. It took me about a year of gaining weight and packing meals to realize this was never going to work for me.

That Group That Accepts They Are Fat And Wants You To Too

This is so dumb and unnessacessary. I do not, nor have ever, understood fat acceptance. They have been reborn in many forms. Body positivity was hijacked by these people. They even took over health being more important than size and mindful eating.

Not that I care that much about what people want to think. Except these people are in my opinion dangerous. Obesity, not being over weight, but being obese, is a problem, healthwise. It needs to be treated. The health and medical community treats obesity like a cosmetic issue and attitudes really must change if this ideology of being fat is a cosmetic problem will change. The fat acceptance movement undermines finding solutions to this problem.Instead, it exposes being whatever size you are "naturally" ignoring that medical conditions cause obesity. Disease may be natural, but it is not desirable.

Of course they don't want solutions, and that's ok. I don't begrudge them this. I would not force a cancer patient into treatment. But I would want them to be able to have the option. And I would not want them to be able to make choices for me if I should be sick. Some of us would like options to help with our obesity. Dare I say most of us who are obese?

The thing I really have never liked about this group is the smugness. I don't get it. Not only are many of the members smug, many of the ex-members are smug as well.

Being obese is not a choice, I'll give them that. It's a complicated dance of choice and circumstances. It's hard and unravelling what causes it is difficult enough with all the bias that exists as it is. All I can do is hope these people learn to show the respect that they would like others to give them.

It is hell to be made fun of for the way you look. It's just not right. Jerks suck. Just because people are jerks to you, don't be a jerk back. Come on.

No one wants to walk into the doctor and hear the obvious and unhelpful, "you need to lose weight."

What needs to happen is a change. The words that come out of the doctor's mouth need to be, "Why is your weight like this?"

Fight for answers.

Being obese is pure miseray for me. Maybe it's a poetic life of beauty for some. Great. That's amazing. But I'm pretty sure most of us would like to be normal and not have diabesity. Accept that we need more medical treatment options for it.

The New Group

A few years ago I went to a group for eating disorders. There was much to be learned there. Since then I have not binged, but I am far from cured. I am better. Now I will be starting a new group. One week from now I will begin.

The first meeting happened. What exactly I was expecting I'm not sure. It seems ok, and it's bigger than I thought it would be. The counselor is nice, the ideas are good, but something seems less than exciting. There is just no other way to put it. Perhaps it's because I've already been doing some of the things we are going to do. Or it might be that I made a commitment to not weigh myself for the duration of the class. This makes me relieved and worried at the same time. I know it's going to be better for me.

One thing I learned from the first meeting is that I do this, I go to food, because it's easy. That is such an odd reason to keep doing something. The whole experience was just a little bit meh. Not sure what to expect from myself or intuitive eating.

Someone in the group today said they love food. I'm pretty sure they meant it. Food is such a monster, beautiful and terrible as the dawn. There is no love, and I do despise it. How can anyone love food? Eating, I can understand people loving this, but not food. It causes me too much misery.

The next day and I'm still thinking about yesterday's group. It was hard to work today. All I wanted to do was think and learn about intuitive eating. Lord.

Hunger is in me. It hit my stomach hard.

I had to take care of some things. That meant ignoring my hunger. The signal sort of diminished. It does come and go in waves. Even as I was preparing my food I lost that edge. Being busy takes away from my body wisdom. I need a moment to shut out the world and just think about what I need.

Pleasant hunger vs primal hunger. Interesting thoughts. The thing I have noticed about all that works is that it doesn't do as much as I want it to. Then I feel like giving up. Learning to accept the success I am given instead of abandoning what I have is hard. In truth I will never be a size 2.

What is this body/food congruence?

Part of me is dying inside. But the only time I was ever at the right weight I was eating like this. Sorta. At least pretty close to this. Thinking about how food makes me feel, not just how it tastes, not being able to even taste it when I do eat it, suffering, guilt, so much turmoil wrapped up in such a natural act.

It is amazing how fast meh can turn to intrigue.

What is honoring hunger? I have a feeling it's not controlling it. Right now, I'm hungry. It's one of those moments when I cannot eat but the feeling is so strong. It will pass, or at least diminish.

How can I honor this?

The feeling is passing me by. It's like it's moving through me. There will be many hours before I can eat. Sorry hunger. I did not take the best care of you. I'll try and do better.

Hunger serves a purpose. It's a scale that helps to gauge energy needs. No matter how much stored energy I have, it comes daily. The body screams to eat. There is a reason for this.
The hunger I feel right now is not unpleasant. It's not bad. My attention is shifted to it, all my other worries are fading as my focus is shifting to it. Being a little hungry relieves my anxiety a little. This eating disorder of mine seems to be morphing a little. Using hunger to relieve discomfort by shifting thoughts is not honoring hunger. It's fading a little again. By the time I can eat I will pick something I really want. I think that will be a way of honoring it. I will use my hunger as information and not ignore it. Still, I must be careful with this. There is some pleasure in emptiness.

When I got a moment to eat my hunger was not that strong. All the places I could go and get food flashed before my eyes. I gave myself permission to eat whatever I wanted. The first thought I had was McDonald's, but I really didn't want that. Then I just went blank. Nothing at all came to mind. All the foods that I could eat seemed so overwhelming, it was too much.

Just to find what I wanted to eat took some effort. All the chatter and images flooding my mind had to be calmed. Then I just took a breath and thought, "What do I really want to eat?'

The answer was steak and cherries. That is what I purchased even though I would have to cook the steaks. In between cooking time I ate some cheese and had the cherries. The hunger is still there just a little bit. The hunger was honored a little today. This is going to be a hard skill to learn.

I'm only on Wednesday. I've watched several videos and ordered two books. Wonder what next Monday is going to bring.

The group met again. It was the second one. This time I just felt numb. Mostly I listened as the others talked. Most of them are much younger than I am. It really drained me. What exactly is dieting? Everything has to go, even tracking what I eat. There is no group next week. It's a much needed break. The work is global.

The control is strong. Talk of educating others was rancid. So wrong. Talk of buying bigger clothes, larger numbers on scales. Are we making progress?

The struggle is balance. Peace comes from finding something unique for me, not controlling others' eating. This is madness. We are talking about what I have been working on. The hook that got me. Honoring hunger. Accepting thoughts. Changing language. What do I really want?

The white bear-don't think about the white bear. The subconscious feeds off of images.

A lot of Annas are using pot to get better. Hunger is very pleasant. I don't understand this scale. I know when I'm hungry and how hungry I get, but there is no unpleasantness with extreme hunger unless I'm really thin and need food.

Everyone was talking about gaining weight. It made me feel like stopping this, like I needed to control my eating. Being overweight is not healthy. Giving up one monster and inviting in another is not what I want. The need for peace and harmony isn't one for pain and suffering. What I want is to be healthy, eat well, deal with discomfort well, and be balanced. My stomach is a little too full. It's late and I'd like to eat away my fears. It's been so long, months, since I've blitzed through food. I'm happier this way. So even if I don't lose weight I'll be happy with intuitive eating. However, I'm not going to be ok if I start gaining. No.

The group is not full of people like me. It has people with similar problems, but they acquired them through different means and for different reasons. The others need to control things a lot more than I do. It's weird to listen to them. It's like when I first realized that not everyone in the first group binged. My problems are unique. One of them brought up a book by an author I find very troubling. That she finds it comforting shows how very different our issues are. Our eating problems come from different places. They talk about society and messages. These are things I don't care about. I care about freedom and finding peace. My oddness is getting in the way of being part of them. I really don't want to be part of them. There is just no way. I have my own problems, I don't want to give them or take on theirs.

Binging and Overeating

When I was a child I could eat a lot of food. Going between my parents and grandparents set me up for a feast and famine existence, but I wouldn't say I was ever out of control. Even when I was eating copious amounts of food I could stop.

Once I turned 12 food got scarce more often. Again, I don't think that my eating was normal by any means, but I didn't have crazy binges. Not yet.

The binging started slowly. I can remember losing control for the first time. It started like a normal overeating session but something changed. I couldn't stop.

A binge is a strange thing. Sometimes I would plan it, thinking about what I would eat for days. Once I had acquired the food I'd go. The fun of it all would end after the first few bites. Then I would want to stop, but a demon would push me on. Sometimes I'd eat everything there was to eat. At times I would be so full my heart would beat fast and my chest would be tight.

Something strange would happen to my body. My stomach would relax and the food would just never fill it. A bad binge might last an hour, but most would be over in a matter of 30 minutes or less. The discomfort would last for hours afterwards. Sometimes I would exercise right after hoping to get rid of the calories. Sometimes I used the discomfort to take my mind away from distressing thoughts.

A group and some hard work later and I quit binging. But now I still overeat. The amount of food is much less and I have more control now, but it's not healthy. I can eat so fast that I don't even taste what I'm eating. This has also been reduced, but I still do it a little.

This eating style is expensive, gross, and very disturbing. Still, it serves a purpose. It takes my mind away from emotions. It takes my thoughts from more distressing ones. But the price is too high. I hated binging, and overeating is not that much better. Every day I get a little better at managing it. That's all I can do, and that is enough.

Unconditional Self Respect and Hara Hochi Bun Me

There is no way I am going to be madly in love with myself. However, I can give respect to just about anybody, even myself. As a self respecting person I can feed myself well.

One of the more interesting things that I have stumbled upon is an ancient idea of being 80% full. Cultivating this feeling is something I'm working on. In India meals were in balance at one third liquid, one third food, and one third empty. I like formulas.

There is power in intuitive eating. Food is in my house, the kind I cannot be trusted with. I cut myself a huge piece of chocolate and was making plans for the caramel next. Sitting down with my big piece of chocolate I started in. It was nice, not as anxiety provoking as usual. It's only food after all.

Something happened as I ate. I realized I had enough. The taste of the chocolate even registered on my tongue. It wasn't lots of fun, like drinking a soda, but not bad.

Still need to work on getting to that 80% full goal. It's actually calming to stop eating when the signal to stop hits. Normally I just ignore my internal signals. Respecting them, unconditionally, weight gain or not, is going to be the road to peace. Maybe I'm just built to be obese. It doesn't feel bad. Now I think what I can do is more important than how I look.

Mother

This is the place where I find myself thinking about the cross road of my life. What made my life weird and made me so strange inside. It was Mother. Even in death she reaches out from her crypt and festers in my mind. That bitch. There was hardly anything she could do right. Such a crazy tempest of a woman.

This really is going to take a long time to unpack. It took so very long to bury, now it's time for an autopsy I suppose. There are things that should stay dead. Hard to know exactly what to do with the bones of the trauma. Some scars and pains hide deep in the past. It doesn't seem like it should matter. How can such things still hold power?

She did a lot. Feelings that come up with the thought of her are the worst kind. Lately the time she tried to kill me is surfacing. It really makes me angry. That day was stormy. For a long time leading up to that day the beast was talking about how in heaven Jesus would have a house for us. A perfect house, one for me, one for my brother, and one for her. Side by side we would live together forever. Then she tried to find the perfect place to park. Storms came and went. Then one day, everything came together.

It was just beyond the yacht harbor, a neighborhood beach with a long jetty. The waves were high and the water was gray. She told us to go out on the rocks. So we did, I led the way. My brother is not stupid, so he turned around when the water started to break over our heads. Like the coward it was, the beast turned back with him. That left me alone on the rocks.

It was a very spiritual moment, fueled by anger. The anger was red hot to the point I didn't feel cold. There is a rhythm to the ocean and I could inch my way along the rocks, hold on long just before I anticipated the water to cover me. It pulled on me a little as I went back, but the sea and I are good friends. The connection I have to the water is almost like love. I knew I was safe. But I also knew that the beast had tricked me. This was a plan to go check out the real estate in heaven.

It was a long way back. The whole way back I watched them waiting on the beach. Every wave made me feel stronger and madder. It stung my hands and the way I held onto the rocks was beyond pain. It was almost an enjoyable pain. When I made my way off the rocks and onto the concrete retaining wall I started to have an epic fit. Wet and awful I was crying and spitting out accusations. The beast had left me to die. All it could say was, "I needed to stay with your brother. I knew you would be ok."

Pure lies.

I would really love to yell at it about this. That would give me some satisfaction. Watch it squirm while I bombard it with the truth. I hated that.

What kind of woman was the beast? A very tragic one indeed. Very charming, smart, not hard to look at, and a fun sort of person. The kind who needed to be the center of attention. At all times. It was tiresome to be around her. I can remember her screaming at me, "You're not smarter than me," over and over when I was eight.

Yes I was.

I think God may have liked her better than me. Lucifer was his favorite angel. There were a few times that she made references to ArchAngel Michael and me. And to be clear she was afraid of me. Once she told me that I was abnormal. That people like me were the ones who survived prison camps by overthrowing the guards at night. The other side of me reminded her of Loki. She bought me a book of Norse Myths because she found this so funny.

All my life she told me how much of a personal embarrassment my appearance was to her. Often she would show me pictures of what a "proper" little girl looked like. That would be tiny with curly hair. Very thin and with a sweet face. The beast often described me as being built like a linebacker. Obviously I did this to spite her.

When I was at a checkup the doctor did my weight and height chart. I don't remember much about that other than he said I would be taller than my dad. I liked that. The beast was furious. When we got home I was measured over and over again. That was when food started to become a problem at home.

In a strange kind of debate the beast would tell me all the reasons why I should not be tall. Tall girls don't get married. My answer was that's alright, I wasn't interested in that. Tall girls get picked on. That was alright too, because I would look scary. Tall girls had a whole lot of problems that sounded pretty good to me. All the beast could do was frown.

As I look at photos pf myself from that time I see a big kid, on the heavy side, but not obese. That came later.

When I was at my grandparents it was a food free for all. Eat what you want when you want. Ice cream, sandwiches, and everyday my grandma made cookies. Everyday. I have fond memories of making chili with my grandpa. Each time he would forget to take the tomato seeds out. Lunch was usually cheeseburgers and fries. I spent a lot of time there. My grandpa was the only person I told about my "midnight snacks." I had started to get up in the middle of the night and make cheese sandwiches at home.

This went on until I hit 12. THen my mother left my dad and split from her family. She isolated us. Then eating got even more bizarre. When not at school we would only eat once a day, after 8pm. Of course that was when there was food. Some days there were some days there wasn't. When I was in 8th grade the teacher asked how many of us had gone a week without eating and I was the only one who raised a hand. I'm not certain what was the longest we went without it. No one cared because my brother and I were overweight.

There was one thing we did have: Soda.

The beast would make certain there was some soda because she wanted there to be some for her. Most of the days we were without she would be gone, God knows where. At these times we would not go anywhere. Missing school was nothing new for us. I don't think we went a full week since I started kindergarten.

The beast was out of control. Dad would bring food once a week, but that would be gone within a few days. The money he gave the beast would be blown on vodka and mysterious things that she did when she left. Usually the beast returned at night. That was the reason there would be soda.

Soda was my life blood. Enjoying food is difficult, but I love soda. I drink diet. That I enjoy. A lot. My tummy doesn't like it though.

This weird eat three days a week, soda only some, would last until I was 16. Then regular eating became important because of the weight loss group. For that I owe them. My disordered eating did get worse, but I don't blame them for that. It was what the time had for me.

Of all the good and bad that happened to me growing up, the food was the most damaging. My uncle would give my family National Geographic subscriptions each Christmas and I would learn about hunger all over the world. One story about mothers watering down formula particularly stuck with me. If I could find a way to take away this kind of suffering, I would. No one should have to be hungry. It's just so hard. It might be a simple joy to have a full belly, but it is one of the best feelings.

There is so much power in the ordinary. These are the things that give us the most joy and the most fulfilment. Wish I could be more ordinary. I think I blend in well on the outside fairly well, mostly. But I know that my experience and my brain keep me from being part of this ilk.

All the beautiful moments in my life have been so ordinary they hurt. Giving birth, hiking deep into the forest. Climbing over rocks. Wading into the ocean and listening to my grandpa talk. The things I value the most are the little things that anyone should take for granted. Ordinary is where the magic dwells. Being odd is hard.

One might ask me if I have ever forgiven the beast. In short, yes, I did. But that didn't dispel all of the anger and the memories bubble up at times.

Forgiveness is a complicated thing. I learned that it is letting go, but on a higher level. This is an act that requires someone to want to receive it, to ask for it. When she did ask, I gave it. Not for her, but for myself. Forgetting is a whole different world.

The greatest, most wonderful Feeling I ever had was when she died. Not that I was rejoicing in her death. I didn't even know that she had passed on. That was a day in early October that I will never forget. On my way to vote in a recall election a feeling just came over me. It was around 11 am and I was in my car driving down the road. The feeling was a release, a feeling of pure sunlight and joy that is beyond words. It lasted less than an instant at it's full intensity but has stayed with me ever since. When I got home I found out my mother had died. At that time.

Finding out she had gone was sobering and dampened the feeling in the light of all the pain my brother was feeling. The unfairness and frailty of life was coming down on him. I'll never forget his words. "I'll miss her."

I will not miss her. But I will say that of all the things the beast has done, that parting gift made up for much of it. If only she would have shared some of it with my brother. It's not fair that he has the burden of all the pain and none of the relief. If I could give him some of that joy I felt I would, but I fear it would just bring him more pain to think about how happy she was to go.

There might have been horrible pain dealt out by the beast, but there were gifts from the ashes. One morning I found myself with my brother standing outside waiting for our house to blow up. Our beast was raving about how the bombs inside it were going to go off at any moment.

Things had not been going well for many weeks.

That morning I left the house a very materialistic and selfish 13 year old. Waiting for the explosion I came to realize something. Part of me worried about all my possessions that were in the house, but a better part of me was born that day. She knew it would be best if that house did blow up and I had a sane mother instead of nothing happening and I was left with the beast.

Possessions are nothing. Trash that will all rot in time. People matter. I would be more of an ass without her. That's for sure.

If she, the beast, hadn't taken away my food would I be like this? I don't know. It clearly didn't help me. I'm not certain if the beast was the only reason for my eating problems, probably the beast is the main source of them, but I know it is too complicated to just be her. Now that the beast is gone the food problems linger on. This is her greatest legacy.

The Mental

My mental health is an interesting issue. I have two diagnoses, one, the first one, is OCD, and the second is bi-polar, mixed mood, with psychotic features. I would say that I have Bi-ploar with OCD. The magic thinking is very close to psychosis. I don't think they are the same though.

The first time I knew I had some different kind of thinking I was very young, around five. There were stairs that went from the house to the garage. Not many, maybe five and as I was walking down them I recoiled from a thought. A very vivid picture of myself falling down the steps and being hurt came to me. At that instant I knew I had to walk down the stairs, carefully, on the right side. Then I would be ok. Even as this was crossing my mind I knew it was off.

It's tough being crazy.

I find myself wondering what really is wrong with me. I have this weird kind of memory, it works in mysterious ways. My outbursts have been tamed, mostly. So now I am just quirky. I could blame it all on my age, but it's not worse than when I was younger. It's easier to hide.

It's been a long time since I've seen a psychiatrist. Going to talk with one makes me feel strange. I don't know if I want, or need medication. That is what the psychiatrist does, the medicine. Counselors come in different varieties and backgrounds. Different pieces of paper and faces, but essentially they do the same thing.

In my current medical plan groups are the thing. I will be starting a couple. One is for eating, intuitive focus, and the other is for women, us older folks. Part of me wants to cancel all of it and just spend time under blankets.

The counselor I saw seems to get me. That's a plus, sometimes finding a good fit is difficult. So far I've found a couple that are going to work. But who knows about the group dynamics. It should be interesting. This is a journey and I hope it will take me to a good place. There might be a few shadows to go through on the way. Places full of anger, shame, and unpleasant moments.

I met with the psychiatrist today. She was nice, and there was a trainee. Hope i didn't scare him. So much history, for me, the beast, and the family. It's been a long time, but I'm starting some medication again. Not a lot, but still, I think I need something to break the cycle. The whirlpool of my thoughts are like a tidal force. A little help in holding them back is nice. Instead of the usual treadmill, my mind feels like it is floating and free.

It's been about a week since I started taking medicine again. Things are slow. I'm tired. This is supposed to get better, but it's really not something that is intolerable. I can manage it. There are good things that have come with the pills. And some very bad things.

It's good, maybe wonderful, that I am not eating like a maniac at night. I take two little pills, one looks like a cloud, the other like a sick sun, and suddenly I'm not thinking about all the things I want to eat. It feels that all the worries just aren't so big. I can sleep. Not that I sleep all night, but I sleep better. This is a relief, and in truth, this is the relief I wanted. It didn't come in like a thunder cloud, more like a drizzle. It was quick and absolute though.

On the other hand it is a reminder that my problems are more organic in nature than I would like them to be. Then there is the fading. After work I feel all used up. My work day is only five and a half hours long. My emotions feel a little stronger, but they still aren't on the surface yet. I can't cry, but I can laugh. Going outside feels weird. It's not that malaise that comes from my own brain, it's something else. I can't put my finger on it.

Being healthy, doing healthy habits is like spinning a great big load stone that is on a bearing. At first it is hard to move, but once it starts spinning it is easy to keep it going. But if it starts to slow down or goes in the other direction, then it becomes a monumental task to get it going in the right direction. I'm trying to get it spinning the right way again.

Today I cried. Just a few tears well up in the sides of my eyes, but it had been years and years since I felt this strongly. At least I felt something strongly that wasn't anger or anxiety. A thought came over me about cooking. These days I find myself watching cooking shows. The culinary arts are not my thing. Never have been, most likely never will be. They do connect me to my grandma. She loved cooking. That made me cry a little.

Thinking back to harder times is so unpleasant. To the outside world I suppose I don't look like such a mess any more but this was not always the case. Not that the full extent of my crazy has ever been completely visible to the public. But in the past pieces of me used to peek out now and then. That was when I was able to b e more in touch with the truth.

It's been a long time since I felt like killing myself. The feeling is still fresh in my mind though. That ache, a longing to just get it all over with. To end all the suffering and the pain. Seems so dramatic now. Even as I feel it I am removed from it.

Even when I had food every day I still thought about killing myself. I actually would fantasize about it constantly. Slowly this was replaced with the numbers of weight loss. The switch happened very slowly. When I was 16 I had this kit I carried with me. I'm not sure when I stopped carrying it or what happened to it.

My safety candles and fancy knife were replaced by my food logs. In those days I often travelled with my great grandfather's

WWI bayonet. But that was for defense, not self harm. Other than he fought in Germany with it I don't know much about how he used it. Then it was passed down to my Uncle John who used it to kill gophers. My brother got it next, who lent it to me when I went on my lone walks.

On those walks I would pretend I was running away from something. A prison camp where I was being held by evil overlords. The overlords were trying to keep my fat so they could keep me in the mines. Now I walk to clear my mind and let thoughts flow.

I had a mental exercise to do. It was watching a video of leaves going down a stream. The leaves were thoughts that were coming and going. I hated that. One of the branches got stuck and wasn't moving. It was really bothering me. My therapist thought it was funny that I wanted to push the branch down the stream. There is a certain way I would like things to be.

As the weeks have gone by I have waited for the novelty of the medication to wear off. It has not. The gaba has not failed me yet. If anything it has made things even easier for me to think. I really do feel better. The uneasiness that nightfall brings has slipped away with winter.

The medication has not really had many side effects. It pushes away the brunt of my fear and makes it manageable to feel. Not that it completely goes away. In the background it lurks like a troll just beyond the light of a fire. But as the fire burns, the troll cannot come near. I sleep well in the safety of that fire.

Therapy

I started therapy instead of just taking a break from dieting. Today was the second dose. Very eye opening. The term she used for my eating was called "storm eating." It seemed to fit much better than compulsive eating. When I do this I feel such urgency and I can't even taste what I'm eating. There is no pleasure, only a drive to eat as much as I can.

The smell thing came up. Apparently smelling can help me to get rid of those unwanted food thoughts. That was something I had noticed. The fact that there are two distinct triggers to my eating at night was something new. If I see others eating I worry that if I don't eat now, it will be gone. There is also the eating that I am more aware of that takes the place of unsettling thoughts.

I have homework.

The first thing I have to do is set aside some worry time. Take 20 minutes to write down all the worries I can think of. The next day took 20 minutes to add any more I could think of. On the third day I am to categorize the worries into ones I can control and the ones I cannot. Doesn't sound too bad.

The next one is tougher. To slow down and think about eating. I never do this. Being mindful when I eat and not doing anything else.

The last one is where the smelling comes in. When the urge to eat comes, not really hungry from the gut, but mind hunger, then wait 10 minutes. During that 10 minutes smell something that has a very pungent and pleasant odor. I'm going to need a timer.

Today's therapy was just a quick check in. There are questionnaires that I fill out before each visit. My counselor showed me what they are for. It was interesting. They showed my progress. I knew I felt better, but I was surprised at how much the chart showed. Seeing that my numbers had been red and were now green was reassuring. In general I do feel better, less anxious, and just more hopeful. Food is a struggle. It might always be. I don't know. But much like the little fairy in sleeping beauty can't undo the curse, maybe she can soften it.

Now I'm going into another group, for older women. Because that's what I am. An older woman. This stage in my life has a whole support group.

Reading

Home work from therapists includes reading. There are two books that were prescribed, one is called The Worry Cure, and the other is Radical Acceptance. The first one really is me. It's making me think. So many things I have issues with. Reading is thinking.

Tonight's chapter is full of tests. I do not know what a schizoid personality is but I scored high in that. That's making me worry. This book is supposed to cure this. Still, I like the book. It's insightful and fun, if not a little tiresome.

It's been a few days since I've read anything. The book I was reading offended me. Silly sounding, but a test I took scored me high in a schizoid personality type. I don't know what that is, and the book didn't explain that, although it did explain some of the other types. Basically I like to be alone and do things alone. Why is that a problem? I will start to read again tonight.

It's hard to focus.

Reading hasn't been my priority lately. I've picked up the books a few times but the subject seems so heavy I'm not ready to take in more information. Even as I feel stuck I can't pick up the books. They may contain the things I need to find what I need to plan a way out. A mind filled with so much just cannot hold another piece of pain. At least not until something is let go.

I have yet to finish reading the books I have and I want another one. Instead of amassing a big pile of reading material I'm going to wait until I'm finished reading what I have before I get some more. Buying books is a favorite compulsion of mine. I want to have all the knowledge.

F it, I ordered the books.

This is one of those areas I do need to work on. I want all the books. If I lived on top of a library I'd be so happy. Not just any library though. One with all the books. God I love the internet. Someday it will have all the books and my life will be complete.

The books are draining. After reading a few pages I feel sick. It gives me a headache. My mind is outgrowing my brain. There should be a place that a person could go to just learn to be human.

The Little Boat

I had a visualization when I was thinking about my problems with food and eating. There was a boat, I was in it. A little row boat with me and I was under a ton of clear gel. It was heavy and weighing down the boat. The boat was anchored on a rocky coast and there were green natural terraces up a high cliff path. On one of the terraces were a group of very thin and beautiful people. Upat the top of the cliff was a temple. I need to get out of the boat to be with them. Among them is where I belong. All this goop is just keeping me stuck in the boat and a storm is coming. This is my last chance to get out and find my place on the cliff.

Being protected is not a bad thing. But it's hard to get anywhere with all this protection holding me down. I feel like I haven't removed anything. Like I'm still in the boat, still stuck under all that gel. How to get out of the boat and get up the hill is no small puzzle. There is a path. A clear way forward. Obviously I just need to get out of the boat. Why is this so hard then?

My stomach hurts. It's been a long time since I have felt it.

When I first placed the call to the doctor I was expecting to begin some big long arduous journey. Soul searching if you will. A good long examination that should take time, maybe years. Who knows, I might need to trek across India to discover the answers. I've been so watered down. Once I was more pure, more connected with my own truth. The path that wandered up the cliff looked long.

But that's not what happened. My mind is weak and rattled with problems. So instead of getting better at the top of the mountain, I got better by getting out of the boat. Taking medication controls the racing thoughts. It eats away the glue and glop that holds me down. There is no need for revelation. Just solvent and good sleep. Over half the battle is just taking a pill and going outside. Too bad it's not a cure, or an elevator to the top.

A new vision came to me today. Things were going on. A friend was going through a hard time. I really wanted to run away from this situation. Instead, I did what I could. To another friend I said something very rude. I wanted to hide, instead I apologized. Huge steps for the grand avoider that I am.

As the day started to dwindle and the light lost some of its power a thought came to my mind's eye. There was a gate, golden and glowing, made of wrought metal, before me. I opened the door. There were thoughts there, other voices, but no forms, and a table.

At the table there was a chair for me. I felt compelled to take my seat at the table.

Then a feeling came. Not words, but a communication that I could have a wish. I thought to myself, this is what I want. Then I felt all the presences in the room around me, surrounding me with love. It was a great embrace. All the worry of the day was gone. I feel better now.

These daydreams, or visions, or whatever they are, have always been part of my life. Music enhances them. I can see myself doing things or see symbols. It's like watching little movies in my mind. If this is part of mental illness then this is a wonderful perk of it. I enjoy them. Bits of my subconscious peaking through are mixed with intuition, and at times there are spiritual spinklings mixed in.

The lastest vision is of vista. I'm standing on a hill, and there is a long green valley below, and in the distance some tall, rolling hills that look purple and pink. The sun is in the clouds, and the sky is blue. The weather is perfect. It feels like spring.

It's time to take a walk across the valley. It looks pleasant.

It's time to step out of the boat.

Now I'm on the shore and it feels hard to stand. Going forward is slow. I'm like a baby learning to walk. Right now learning to eat is my path to follow.

Limits

This feels good and I know I'm making progress. One thing I must accept is that there will be, and that there are limits. Growth is not endless.

No matter how thin I become I can never be young, no matter how fit I become I will never be strong. I am what I am as Popeye would say. Taking this to heart is very difficult. Sometimes when I realize I cannot achieve my true wish for myself I just give up. Why fight fate?

Accepting is a powerful gift, but it can be so discouraging at the same time. Running the rock up the hill every day brings no joy, but letting go of the rope that suspends brings disaster. It's so hard to know what is acceptance and what is giving up.

Giving up is bad, but knowing your limits is important. Wasting effort chasing after the impossible, giving into futility, is such a soul crusher. But not putting in enough can be even worse.

This is why taking a moment to fully inventory situations is so powerful.

I weighed myself today. It has been a long time since I faced the scale. It said 181.8. That is where I'm at. It's not where I want to be. It brought up some feelings and some questions. I know weighing myself daily is healthy for me. Weighing myself four or five times a day is not so much. Letting it go for months on end can be good or bad depending on why I'm not doing it. Right now I really don't know what I want to do. That's not true, I know what I want to do. I want to obsessively control my weight and get it down as low as I possibly can. That just may not be something I can, or should, do.

Not being good enough is not as bad as fading, which I am starting to do. You may wonder, just what is fading? This is the slow loss of sharpness of my mind. It's hard to notice it's so slight and the brightness of my soul has not been affected. The limits that my mind has imposed on me are growing, in a very tiny way, but in a very real way, year by year. Fading is scary.

Mistakes are scariest of all. I hate making them, and I hate making them in front of people even more. This is one thing I have that balances out this, I am brave. At least to some degree. Avoidant and brave, my soul is a battlefield. My weakness is how strong I am. Knowing that I could do more but don't want to freezes my spirit.

Being busy isn't something that I'm good at. Having free time, time to breathe, to think and dream, and as vital to me as air. Today was a busy day. Things went wrong and yet it wasn't so bad. It was a very human day.

The ups and down were far away and I was limited by what I could do. Car trouble is the insidious disturber of modern life. Follow the car drama with lots of computer work. It makes my mind soggy. The older I get the more limited I feel. Handling these days, and even smooth days, is hard. Just give me a long path and a pair of good shoes. All I want is to clear my mind.

The scale has had to be given a vacation. In order to become more at peace with food I must tune into the body wisdom. Trusting it means that I must not let my eating be guided by the number at the scale, at least not right now. I will rethink going on a weight loss journey after I have better balance in my life.

This weight might be something I just learn to accept. It really depends on my health. If I find that my blood pressure or blood sugar is too high I try to lose some weight. For now I just need to eat like a natural person.

I really love weighing myself and monitoring my weight. The only time I don't do this is when I'm out of control and compulsively eating. Numbers and fun, and I love to count and measure.

The scale needs to be silent for at least two months. How I am worrying about gaining weight during this time. Just being ok with whatever weight I might be as long as I eat normally is going to be hard. Food is so hard.

Avoiding Reality is Bad, But It's Me

When I'm not doing the things I'm supposed to do I don't step on the scale. Whenever I know that something will give me bad feedback I tend to avoid it. Reality can be cruel. Avoiding reality only causes me more anxiety, but the thought of facing said reality peaks my anxiety. This doesn't get relieved by facing it, but it does bring it down.

Being out with friends is not bad. But my anxiety goes up when I go out. I like being out. There are many things I like doing that bring anxiety. I don't know what this is about, but it's the same kind as facing reality.

But that's not the only reason I do the eating game. Some of it is a habit. Unveiling everything is hard.

There are some recurring themes I am seeing. I like easy, not hard. I want a cure, not constant work. There are so many unpleasant things I want to forget, not confront. Being so full of limits is the human way. Time to overcome these.

If only there was a better way to avoid things that cause me pain. I have covers on mirrors and I avoid looking at videos of myself. Wish there was a way to filter out the unpleasant and let me go on about my merry stupid way.

As Seen on TV

Sometimes I watch a lady on YouTube. The reason she fascinates me so is that she has my face and some of my delusions. I see her searching for the cure. Putting her hope in this and that, running back to my favorite group, the first one, and then giving up, because the truth is that there is no cure. In truth she changes diets more often than I change clothes. But that hope stuff propels us on in the face of logic. Why should it work?

I know that all in fervor. It's useless. Why? Because the problem is too complex for a cure, it's got a life of its own, the beast can only be controlled, not killed. The control takes time and baby steps. It's a hard to learn dance that values patience over effort. Being kind over punishment works wonders. I hope she can find the keys to her health, she has many of my problems. It's a tough journey, I don't think I would want to do it in front of an audience.

I see her pouring her heart out and being the butt of people's jokes, I was that once. Being so raw and exposed is not easy as it is, let alone being picked over and berated. I feel for her and I want to slap her. Why does she do it? I know, she needs to feel heard. I did too. She really desperately wants to feel understood and that her light isn't the only one shining in the dark. When she creates things and does that which calms her it brings her up for ridicule. That hurts. Especially when your face is attached. I hope she finds a way to the light in this dark world of ours. People pick her apart because she has something, something special. Keep trying to bring that forth and show the world that sparkle. Shine for us, and dance in your underpants. I'll do the same.

Correctly, she understands that people hate her because she's fat. That bothers her, not because what people think, but because that is why we hate our bodies. It makes the truth sting.

Overreacting

Confrontations kill me. They are just too much. Any little battle brings up so much emotion. A conflict over the smallest thing feels like life and death. There is something inside me that starts to boil and I need to rip things.

Eating is so calming at these times. It feels like salvation when I eat. Nothing is as valuable as energy. Food energy is life. The gift of precious spirit. Cupcakes are like rainbows you can hold in your hands. They fit in your tummy. I had a hard day. A lady stole my debit card information and here I am without a cupcake.

Not that what happened is that big a deal. The stress of dealing with cancelling the card, and now I have to dispute a charge wears on me. Really I'd like for someone to pay for this. The criminal won't. She will pretend it's a mistake, oh silly her, and nothing will happen to her. All I can do is not go back to the place and use cash in similar situations. A cupcake won't help me.

Being upset is very uncomfortable. Calming myself is hard. The wave of anger is so hard to control. If only things could just be smooth and easy. I think I've grown enough as a person in this category. God please send less confrontation my way.

Repetition

Lord, another cycle begins. It's so old. Why do I do this? If I just stopped then I would be fine. Of course if I stopped then I would have to do something else, or nothing. The food is the devil I know.

I had a long day. There was no time for me. Examining it, there were some times I could have set some boundaries that would have made sense. People around me were having bad days. They were asking a lot of me and draining me.

Talking about their problems and texting me at work isn't unreasonable. It's just there are a bunch of people all at once. Everyone wants something. I can't give everything they want. It's very frustrating and I want some time for myself. Days when I don't have a free minute make me anxious.

I'm really not sure how better to handle this. People are still having trouble and I'm going to have to deal with them in the future. But not like today. That gives me a little relief. The thought that there may not be a solution to this kind of problem is not easy for me to handle.

Constantly I go back to worrying about food. It makes all the other thoughts and fears so small. Round and round. Am I hungry? Did I eat the right food? Too much? Should I be ashamed? So much easier to worry about this than other things. The minute I eat I get relief. The thoughts bring a different anxiety that changes my thoughts and feelings. These are not pleasant thoughts and feelings, but they are not as difficult as the ones they replaced.

This is like trying to get from my home in California to my brother's in Texas via the Merry-Go-Round.

Once again I did not enjoy eating. This is so hard for me to do. Life in a body is tricky. The body doesn't come with a manual, it comes with wisdom of sorts. Some of the signals it gives can get mixed up. Not all of us get bodies that are in tip top shape. Learning to respect and care for it is hard enough without sabotaging my eating.

Another rough day of demands. On the way home from work a battle waged in my mind. I stopped at McDonald's. This is the home of warm and magical memories. So much stress was on me and I drove through. Before I made the turn in the driveway I lost the first battle. The second wave came when I saw the menu. This time I did better. Although I could have turned out of line before I got to the place where I placed the order. There a compromise was struck.

Medium fries, two regular cheeseburgers and a diet coke was my order. I ate the fries, and one of the burgers.

The food was cold and tasteless. But the memories were so brilliant. It was eating in the car big fun. The food didn't matter. It was almost like ghosts of those I loved were driving down the roads with me. My phone was full of messages that interrupted me.

The taste of the food didn't matter. It was fueling old memories when I was important. Times when I mattered and had no one making my life hard.

That was an interesting thought. When I was going to McDonald's as a child it was for me. My choice and all I could eat. These lunches with my grandparents are still some of the best of my life. This was the beginning of this cycle. McDonald's and sneaking cheese and wonder bread.

Other people are difficult to deal with for me. I like them, and I care about them. Still, I just don't like to be around people that much. Family is enough for me. When I was 26 my grandma said something like this to me. Maybe I'm like her. Sometimes I wonder how I can strike a balance in my life that will make me happy. Then again, that's not what I want.

All is never lost though. There is always tomorrow and that is when I will start all over again. Buy me a ticket for that ride. I want to sit on the zebra this time. No matter how many times I end up in the same place I still believe in the power of the merry-go-round. It moves so it must take me somewhere someday.

Moments of Opportunity

There are times, brief pieces in time, when things become clear and the power to make choices is available. These are not easy choices, but they are times when I am more in control than on autopilot.

Today was one of those little fragments of time. It was a busy day. Not super busy, still, there was much to be done. Things came up here and there. It all got done. This did not leave a long time to contemplate my health.

These moments are fleeting, they don't last long. They need to be nurtured and grown. If they are caught, held on to, and tended to, they just go.

Being at the crossroads can last an instant. Sometimes picking up one chocolate can make the difference between weeks of suffering or health. It's so weird that these little, tiny, and conscious movements can lead to such places.

Like falling asleep on a bus. If you get on the wrong one you can wake up miles from where you want to be. Being more mindful of these actions, making the right choices at these pivotal points, is the magic I need in my life right now.

The Worry Game

I am the Queen Of Worryland. Part of my road to healing my heart is giving up my crown. Today was step one. I took 20 minutes to just write down all of the worries I have. It was interesting letting them flow instead of trying to fight them back. There wasn't really a time when they didn't stop coming, but they did slow down. Now it's later and I don't feel so anxious.

It really is amazing all that's on my mind. I'm not looking forward to doing the 20 minutes of worrying again. Makes me a little anxious and I would like to just goof off. Worrying makes me think about all those things that I really should be doing right now.

Many of my worries are long past gone. Things that are not likely to happen again. Still these events are haunting me in the background of my mind. This is a barrier between me and my feelings.

Finding time to conscientiously worry is not easy for me. I don't want to do it. Worry makes me feel small and powerless. The daydreams I have make me feel happy and powerful. Purposely thinking about things that I spend effort to avoid is very unnatural. The uncertainty of the weeks that are coming are hard enough to think about. Thoughts break into my happy time. Inviting them to dwell in my mind is painful and like taking a hot piece of iron in hand.

Worry is starting to be under control.

Secrets

So much of my life I kept everything to myself. Then I let out too much. When my child was old enough to have something to talk through I got her a counselor. Outloud she wondered why it wasn't ok to share all her problems with the world. To this I said, "There is nothing wrong with your body, but you don't need to walk around naked all the time."

It's a fine line between privacy and secrecy. One is the foundation of health and the other is the poison that kills. Walking that line is hard. I suppose it's better to let out something and regret it then to be forced to keep something in. It's good to have trusted souls to confide in. If what they believe or not isn't important, the truth doesn't care what people think. Just having someone there while your soul is being laid out in the darkness is all that is needed. No comments or judgement. Fellowship.

The food has been a long time private part of my life. It was a secret when I was young. Pieces of it are secret now. Sharing all of this laying it bare before God and man is not an easy choice. The only reason I've done this is for those who come after me.

My grandmother was always full of good advice. Some of her words have been the compass that have guided my life by. When she got cancer I went to see her and she had something to tell me. I thought it was going to be something about life or death. Instead she was excited that she was under 200 pounds.

There is something more than just conditioning in my habits. Not only was my grandmother obsessed with her weight, she was obsessed with food. Even on a filbert orchard food was scarce during the depression.

Our minds are wired a certain way. I hope sharing this will be like providing a map for the future generations. Don't suffer, get that eating in order before worrying about anything else. It's a gift.

That Time I Didn't Cure Diabetes

Many years ago, I can still remember it so clearly, I was diagnosed with type II diabetes. This did not bother me because I was going to cure it.

At the time I weighed 265. So if I lose 100 pounds then voila, no more diabetes. The look on my doctor's face when I explained this was telling. Nevertheless I was determined. I was going to get cured.

When one develops type II diabetes losing weight becomes a different sort of activity. Instead of it coming off like when I was 16 it didn't move. At least not easily. There were new strategies to try.

Over the years I have been able to chip away at that number. It goes up and down, but it doesn't stay 265. It's much lower right now. So I should be cured.

My diabetes doesn't care about my cure, it is much, much worse than when I was first diagnosed. Now I am on insulin. So if I'm eating better and my weight isn't as high, why am I not cured?

Because the short answer is that obesity doesn't cause type II diabetes, insulin resistance does. It probably causes obesity too. At the very least it contributes. So just lowering weight is not enough to cure.

It's the carbs and the insulin. This is a disease and it gets worse over time.

Today was not a great food choice day. I had cake and before that I took a shot of murder. Giving myself the death shot makes me nervous. It's a tough choice. Eat the cake and skip the shot, or skip eating the cake are the least anxiety causing choices. Today I went to have the cake and take the liquid death. The worry really does dissipate. It's magic. I was able to enjoy the cake a little. At least the smell. Maybe that's what I can start with. Enjoying smells of food. Ease into eating more mindfully. Watch that blood sugar more carefully because there is no cure coming anytime soon.

Food Diaries, Numbers, Calories, Oh My

I like tracking what I eat. Measuring and weighing food is fun for me. The numbers game of weight loss is fun, but it never works. Some numbers do. But as far as figuring out how much to cut out to lose a certain amount of weight there is no way. Nature does what nature feels like doing. Nature cares not for numbers.

It's been a while since I tracked my food. I've tried to do it in a more loose fashion but I hate that. Writing down onces and exact amounts is so satisfying. It goes back to the first days of the group. Tracking what I ate was part of my salvation. I had a food diary and I didn't trust that they would give me a new one each week. I kept it on my refrigerator and followed the suggestions each day. Only after I had amassed a month's worth did I start to write on them.

Body Wisdom - Body Trust

I don't trust my body. Today I ate while doing nothing else. Paid attention to the food and all the sensations that went along with that. It was so hard. My mind kept thinking about other things.

After I ate I wanted more but instead I thought about how I felt. It had taken a long time to eat. Much longer than normal. So I could tell that I felt full. Part of me was trying to figure out the numbers, or about how many calories I had consumed, and that was a hard train of thought to stop.

Waiting to eat until I was hungry was another tough ordeal. Now I must wait to eat again until I need to, when my stomach is calling me, not my anxiety.

The stomach hunger vs the head hunger is not hard for me to tell the difference between. Funny, controlling myself when the stomach hunger hits is pretty easy. It's that head hunger that gets me.. So perhaps this is good evidence that the body wisdom may have an advantage over logic.

For two meals I ate mindfully. There were no distractions and I thought about each bite. It is around 5:30pm and I am not going to eat again. Honestly I feel so good. It's hard to believe that I torture myself for no reason. Being so conscious to let the unconscious take over is weird. Guess I've overridden it so much it's hard to let autopilot fly the plane.

My tummy is not happy.

Almost ate to the TV today. Caught myself mid bite. It was during a cheese and avocado meal. Something about cheese is hard. That taste and smell reminds me of being small. It's the exact kind I would eat at my grandparents. The most bitter sweet food of them all. There is a cheddar I have found I know my grandpa would love. I will never get to share it with him. Right now I don't have any of it.

Something about that smell of sharp cheddar makes me feel so happy. A song by twenty one pilots is playing in my mind. The kitten is trying to get my attention. Wish I could turn back time.

Fighting the urge to eat not hunger. It's harder to fight the urge. Now it the time when I can eat. I'm not hungry. Still, I feel like eating. This feels more than just a habit. Eating is comfortable. Today is a dark and cold dreary Monday. Something warm in my tummy would be nice. But I'm going to wait until I actually feel hunger. So hard.

Last night I had a snack late at night. That's interfering with my hunger signals. It wasn't a big deal kind of snack but I'm paying a price for it right now. The choices I made last night are cascading into my morning. It's something to think about.

Finally got a stomach rumble. Can't say I really feel hungry, but the noise is pretty loud. There is a hollow sort of feeling inside me as well. Next break I will eat something and drink some hot tea. Not being able to just eat whenever is one of those adjustments humans in a body must make. Being that hungry was the spice that made the food good. I feel great. Listening to my stomach after ignoring it for so long is difficult.

One interesting side effect is that I am starting to enjoy eating. There is still dread at the thought of eating, but it's not as bad. Better is happening.

There is a way to lose weight, a feeling. If I keep my satisfaction at a certain level, I will get to a more healthy weight. Words have power and I need to change them. No more weight loss. It needs to be all about health. It's going to take some time to change my vocabulary. Even more time to believe. Already I can feel an army rising up in my mind to rebel against this. Letting go of the old ways is going to be hard.

Why Giving Up Dieting Made Me Cry

The thought of step one of Intuitive Eating brought up a wall. The thought of going through yet another round of counseling turned my mind numb. There was something just underneath the surface that I hadn't touched before. Something that I didn't want to give up. With the tears came the realization of what it was like way back on that first diet. That was freedom and control.

The first time I went on a diet I was rebelling against abuse. Calling it out. Demanding to eat everyday and taking control of my body. It was empowering. Damaging for certain, but more positive than negative.

Getting back to that boat imagery. That would be my diet, it took me away from my prison. It saved me from the abusive world of my mother. Now that I've got my own control over what I eat do I really need to control it so much?

I had no idea how much power I found when I started to diet. At least I didn't remember it. Going back to the beginning reminded me how wonderful it felt to move away from the beast. Part of becoming myself was being able to have food every day. The dieting made that possible. With the deprivation came regularity.

As I grew older I had more and more control over my food and my body. Most of the time I was holding on to dieting. Now it makes sense. It was through the diet that I had security. Bingeing became more intense as the food rules tightened up.

So now my life boat has become an unwanted stress.

Getting out of the boat is giving up the diets, giving up losing weight, and stop having so many rules around eating. I've made it to the shore.

The Queen

If I am no longer in charge of my body then what exactly is starting to go on? It feels like a revolution has begun. Something has been disposed of and there is a void left in her place. The legitimacy of my reign over my desires. Not that I am giving over to complete abandon. The queen is dead, or at least in hiding.

No one is as good at denying their needs as I. When I was younger I could hold my breath the longest. My tolerance for pain is very high. Perhaps I am not the most starving person in the world.

That battle cry to lose weight and eat right is starting to lose its strength. No force has ever worked, the slow and simple way has always been the one that took me where I needed to go.

The simple, the ordinary. Trust in the body, it doesn't need a keeper. So much uncharted territory in this old body. I thought we had the bulk of the problem well at hand. Now what? I wonder.

I Am So Fat

There is an empty feeling inside my body. It feels so good. This is the only way I can feel thin. I love this feeling. The bumps on my back and lumps on my stomach are so offensive to my sensibilities. Being fat sucks.

When I am hungry, from inside, I feel light. It's scary and brings back old feelings. The strongest feeling is being in control. Not feeding my body makes me feel less stuck to it. It's like watching a movie instead of living.

I shouldn't hate my body, but I do. Nothing about it is the way I want it to be. From the shape of my face to the depth of my belly button I feel all wrong. Sometimes I think I'm in someone else's flesh. Mine should not be this big and so flawed.

At this moment in time I have no idea how much I weigh. At least not down to the pound. That is somewhat worrisome. The bumps on my back just above my waist tell me that I need to lose weight. The way my pants feel screams keep the mouth shut.

With all that being true I feel so good right now. Eating has become less of a furtive intrusion and just a normal passing. My belly button is not a pit of shame. I do want to enjoy the simple joys of food and my flesh.

I am just dying to step on the scale. Every morning I see it in the corner of the bathroom mocking me. Eating when I'm hungry and giving control of my weight to nature is so unsatisfying. Giving up the reins feels wrong. There are some things that are better left to chance. Part of weight is just in the DNA. If only I could edit my DNA, just a little.

I don't want to be fat.

Getting Stuff Done

There are many things that I would like to do. Things that would make me happy and things that I should do. Instead I just do the minimum that I must do to survive instead. If only I could stop doing this. I need a plan.

Today I took a step. It was a very small one. I bought highlighters and printed out 10 pages of a manuscript I wrote. Over the next few months I plan to edit this manuscript and finish writing the bones of another manuscript to share with another. Those are my goals. By summer I want to be onto something new. It's time to clean up all the unfinished work I have. Then I will feel complete.

Procrastination is my favorite thing. Writing is so much fun. Cleaning it up is not my favorite. A body cannot survive on dessert, and a mind cannot only create. Polish is important as well.

Easy Is Hard

Being in a circle of illusions is easy. Breaking free is not. It is time to take stock of myself and decide what I really want to do. This isn't so much fun. Getting going is hard. Worse, I might need help. Everything wonderful usually does take a group effort. Yet I like to work alone. Melding minds and coming to understandings are so difficult. Where is my easy living?

Peace is hard work. It sounds counterintuitive. Peacefulness should be easy, not full of toil and tribulation. To get to the peaceful garden I have to climb a wall of broken glass. Scaling it to the place where my mind can rest and be free is going to leave scars. Opening up old hurts seems so unnessaccary. I thought I was over all of it. But that past still holds me as strongly as the now. I feel so exposed right now.

Hunger - R E S P E C T the Feeling

Hunger is a tough feeling for me. It is not a simple thing. Food is so valuable that many cues can lead to eating. There is the kind from the gut, deep inside the body, and then there's the kind that comes from ideas. The ideas are the ones that are the hardest kinds of hunger for me to resist.

The body feelings are more real, and while they are urgent, I can control them. The ones from my mind seem to drive me. When I don't really need to eat, that's when I need to learn to control myself. So backward.

Feeling hunger is not hard, this respecting it thing is very strange. An urge to finish the chocolate thing came over me. But I am not hungry. To do so would not be honoring my hunger. If I do eat it then it will be the next time I feel hungry. I feel so fat.

Ultimately respecting hunger signals is respecting my body. That I can see. If I want it to work well, if I want good health, then

I'm going to need to cultivate this respect. Part of that respect means accepting that my body might work better at a larger size.

When I honor my hunger I better notice body signals, naturally. Smells are stronger, and I notice them more. The more I pay attention, the stronger the signals get. They like being heard. Now they break in when I'm doing things I need to focus on. Instead of ignoring my body, I take note. If I can't eat or drink at the moment, I give myself permission to check in with it when I can. The signal strength fades a little after I dismiss it. I am working on paying attention.

Being still and listening to myself makes me feel so good, it's hard to explain. It didn't happen right away. Right now I feel like I'm glowing on the inside. The pit of my being is warm and well. Even after eating I feel light. Today is beautiful.

It's been a few weeks since I've ate to full. Tonight I was so tired and I did it. Being careful, at least at first, paying attention, I knew I wanted more food. Warm food. So that's what I gave myself. I'm not stuffed, but the pressure on my waistline is significant. The hollow feeling is gone and I don't feel light. It makes me feel sleepy and not really good about myself. Part of me wants to eat more. After all, I ate too much, I might as well make it count.

That is not going to happen. Today I'm settling for good enough. Next time I'll stop a little sooner. It would be nice to have some more space left. I'm at 88% full.

There is a problem with my respect for my hunger. I love being hungry. The hungrier I am, the better. I feel light, in control, and superior. If I was thin the discomfort might be painful, but I am overweight. It feels wonderful to starve. This makes fasting hard. I can go for days, but I know I shouldn't. Even for therapy, I need to heal my relationship not only with food, but with hunger, before I can fast.

I've been eating some foods that are not so great for me. My stomach hasn't been the happiest. Truly it's impossible to honor hunger eating foods that are engineered to override hunger signals. That bag of veggie straws messed me up. They were like a gateway drug. Then I had some fast food which made me hungry even after my stomach felt so full. Clearly there are foods that don't work well with intuitive eating.

So I'm going to avoid foods and recipes that are lab created. Fast foods and the things that linger in the middle of the grocery store are going to be looked at with suspicion. Funny, I've given up clean eating, only to sort of return to it in a way.

Walking makes me feel things. After I walk for a week or so I can feel my body signals better. I think I need to focus on making my hunger signals stronger. Picking the right foods and doing the right exercises will help to make my hunger scream at me.

After I ate lunch today I wanted to eat even though I felt full enough. Packing in more seems to be a great idea for some reason.

Luckily I picked foods that send strong fullness signals. Having protein and fat are important as well as watching sugar and salt is key. The food can sabotage those signals that are so precious. Fostering these signals means not only listening for them, but engaging in activities that strengthen them. Food choices are going to be critical to reestablishing good communication with my inner needs.

Words I Would Tell My Past Self

If I could go back in time and have a quiet dinner with my past self, say when I was 20 I would have so much to say. I'm sure that if I took it to heart then, my life now would be so different. Maybe better, maybe not. One thing is for certain, I'd be healthier.

The first piece of advice I would give is to always make time for walking. Even a half an hour. Just go out and walk. Never move to a city you hate, Drive a bit instead. Eat meat, cheese and drink water. Just say no to sugar, It's the white death. Eat fat more often or you'll lose your gallbladder. Gallstones are evil creatures.

Go camping, but take a cot. Go out to the middle of nowhere as often as you can and see the stars. Light pollution poisons the soul.

Being married is overrated. You can have kids without the ceremony. Enjoy your children more and worry less. Go to the beach more often. Money is more important than you think. Find a way to make more of it.

Make a plan. Stop just living day by day and think about what you want and where you want to be. There is more to life than watching it and making fun of it.

Stop fighting who you are and just accept that. Adopt the characteristics you like in others, but don't try and be them. Be a better you. Never be obsessed over other people, make yourself the most amazing person you've ever met.

It's ok to have a belly. Thin people don't live happier lives. Yes, lots of things suck about being us. Just as many things don't. That's just the way it is.

Be good to your brother, he will always be your best friend. Spend more time with your grandparents, you'll miss them when they are gone. Don't forget the relatives that helped you grow up, you'll miss them too. When they leave you will really feel left behind. Send Aunt Almy pictures. You'll regret not doing this.

Try to be productive, and forgive yourself when you can't be. Push passed the pain. It will go away. The brain fog comes in waves. Just do what you can and wait until the next sunny time. No one will help you but your brother. This is a fact.

Swim when you can. Find a quiet place to think. Never give homeless money, only food and water. Try and smile. THink about good things. When you feel helpless, help others. Don't be so touchy, but demand respect by giving it.

Letting Go

That is the art, the act, the thing that really is the last step that gets to the top of the mountain. Letting go of all the weight holding the body back. Being in a body means making peace with tha. Not just accepting it's limits, but using it the way God intended for it to. The dwelling comes with rules that have been handed down through the generations, some have been lost along the way. Some need updating with the times. Most instructions come from deep inside. Our hearts can guide us if we let go.

Even the ideas that we need to let go of can be elusive. Sometimes I don't know what's going on because I am in such a food daze. Worrying about it, thinking about it, and just being distracted by it so I don't have to think about my many, many shortcomings.

The diets must go, all the rules, all the counting, the measuring and the many shoulds and musts. They are not that helpful anymore. I don't need them to take care of myself or to be free. Now I am more than free from things, I'm just free, period.

I don't really want to let go of myself, I want to find myself.

This is the time I like to eat. It's late and I feel a little stressed but not too bad. Unwinding with a cup of tea is nice. There is no food. Others are eating, and I have this urge, but it's hardly more than a whisper. Easy to let it go by. Like those leaves on the stream. The urge is there and then it floats by. Tasting the peach in the tea and drinking it is very enjoyable. The calm it brings is soothing. This is a better way. Not as easy a path to find, but a better one to take. If I can remember how this feels I think I can avoid the over eating.

No Cure, Just Work

This is a journey, a life path, a habit, and mostly, a lot of work. It takes thought. The truth is that as my life goes on, my body changes. And as it goes through its changes, I must adapt. Food needs change. Sometimes I need more, sometimes less. As the years go on, I need less and less carbohydrates.

As long as I live I will need to be a little more mindful of eating than some. It's ok, it's my body and I am its keeper. It might end up being a fat body. As long as it can do what I want I'm willing to accept that. I have come to the realization that my belly button is not the most unsightly of ghastly blights upon my eyes. I think I like it. It's easier to punish myself than it is to like my body. That's just absurd.

Food deserves more respect, and so does my hunger. Respecting is work. Constantly I'm reminding myself to pay attention. The signals are there, everything I need I have. It is a puzzle with all the pieces laid out before more. Only once I put them together a force shifts them apart. It's a never ending task

The fact that I need to wait is the hardest part. If there was more to do or something to punish myself with I would feel like I was making progress. But the truth is that most of taking care of myself is not really that dramatic. It's tedious.

Feeling Better

Time has gone by, a few months. Right now I feel better. Much better. All the therapy, the writing, the different homework, the books, and the medication are working. Things are getting done and I just don't worry about all the things that can go wrong.

I still check the doors and the windows. The oven gets a good going over a few times a day, just in case. Oddly enough I just don't feel as tired. This could be because I am making better food choices. Before I started taking medication I was worried that it would make me sleepy during the day. At first it did, but now I have more energy. Winter just ended. Spring feels so hopeful this year.

Feeling More

The voice is growing. My feelings are showing. Everyone is moving on and I feel alone with my thoughts. It's a beautiful sort of ache. The pain isn't easy. There is just so much I wish wasn't happening. I've made my mistakes, the worst one was not taking in all those joyous moments when my kids were little. Worry has robbed me of so much. How I'd love to crawl under a rock by myself for a few days.

The feeling in the bottom of my stomach is getting stronger than the cravings in my mind. As this change is happening I'm noticing that other feelings are becoming more acute. They are coming in from the now and the past. It is a lot. In between I do feel much better. The weather is nicer, it feels like the whole world is healing.

I Weighed Myself Today

The feelings this brought up were so anxiety fueled. It felt bad. There was no choice about it. I was going to the dentist and had to know my weight for medication dosage. It was exactly what I thought it would be, and not what I wanted it to be. This made me feel like throwing away the intuitive eating. The first thing I thought about was how to lose weight. All the numbers flooded into my mind and the peace I fought for left.

So much is going on right now. I'm not using food to cope. However I'm not a paragon of eating virtue. I'm being human. That's not enough. Really what I want is to effortlessly eat and be perfect.

Tere is this strange mix of hope and desperation inside of me right now. Today I ate some pizza and I want to eat more, but I am not hungry. My stomach is turning. The pizza did not sit well inside of me. It's time to just let go of all that old behavior. But that is such a scary thing to do. Feeling along with my eating has been so hard. It is very healthy though. I'm not giving up. But I am slowing down.

I haven't been regularly weighing myself. Slowly, my weight has crept up. Not by much, but I was hoping for the opposite effect. To weigh or not? Deeply personal, and I think it depends. Sometimes it's too much, sometimes I need to. Right now it's not helpful. Tomorrow, who knows?

Tough Times

It's been a hard week. Many things have taken my energy this week. There is this grinding inside me that wants to just weigh myself. Maybe food could fill up the bad parts inside me. Maybe not.

There are other ways to find out what is going on with my body. There are better ways to handle stress. Instead of eating I talked about the problems I'm having and I tried to walk more. That felt better. Paying attention to how I feel after I eat also took my mind off my discomforting troubles. The strange swirlings in my stomach are just as distracting as chewing.

The rolls of fat that pool at the bottom of my torso are speaking to me. They are not pleasing to me. They feel heavy. My rolls are very squishy. The sky is full of clouds today. The weather can't decide if it should be warm or cold. That reflects my insides right now. Everything is changing and it feels like it's too much.

The turning of my stomach feels comforting right now. I don't need anything. But still I eat. That pit in my stomach was empty. The rolls on my torso can't tell me when to eat. Listening to my stomach is more important than feeling the pockets of pudge on my sides. This battle is so hard. All I want is peace, but at what cost? Do I have to be obese? Just because things are hard does that mean that I should just stop caring about what I eat? My body feels pretty good. That wellness is helping me think better and feel better mentally. Sitting with discomfort and not letting it poison the rest of my life is so hard. Letting go of what my mind says about what I am eating is hard. I've spent so much time learning about food, measuring, weighing, adding, and tracking. Unlearning this is so unnatural. Odd. It's unnatural to just be natural.

If only I could take a break from everything. Just go to an island somewhere and breathe. See the ocean, my old friend, count the waves, build in the sand. Maybe paint a few watercolors. Or just do nothing at all. Anything that doesn't involve staying in bed all day, but is still not very productive.

There is a very human urge to just run away when the going gets tough. Why not? Find some place green and safe. Eat fruit and get fat in the sun. The problem with this? The thoughts, the ghosts, they follow. Dreams turn to nightmares, little doubts grow into anxieties. Pay attention to what seeds you plant. No matter how far you run, the vines and branches can trip you.

The hunger is gone. The turning in my stomach has stopped and it feels like whatever whirlpool was spinning in there has stopped. Things have gone back to sleep. Part of me would like to eat away my fears. This would be disrespectful to my body, to the way it works, what it needs, to my hunger, and ultimately to the food itself. Abusing food is disgusting. So many don't have what they need. Every night I fall asleep with a roof over my head and a full stomach. If it is not full, it's by choice.

My problems are making me sad. Having feelings back is so different. Where did they go? How did they manage to find their way home? Why are the tough ones coming up to the surface first?

The hardest emotion for me is sadness. She is the first one to move back in. It was a slow reunion. It's a sweet unpacking of old bags, but it hurts to have this old guest back.

Having a break from life would be nice. I'd like to see my dad, or just talk to my brother. It's hard being far from my son. Family is the only thing that matters. How I wish I had a few more memories of my grandparents. Sometimes I feel like I live on the moon. Miss the soft earth beneath my toes.

Today was a chocolate day. I'm so tired, all I wanted to eat was just fun food. Peanuts and chocolates and fun. It didn't make me feel very good after I ate it. So tired of doing difficult things. I want food to be easy.

My back is hurting.

It's time for a fast. This can be tricky. I love to fast, and doing it is so healthy for me. But it can trigger eating problems. So I need to watch my thinking. It's easy to get addicted to starving. Fasting is something to be respected, it's a time of rest.

Doldrums

To say that I am apathetic about my health would be just about right. There is no excitement about going forward. Right now I don't want to learn anything. It would be fair to say I don't care. Then again, I really do. Perhaps I'm just tired of it all. Perhaps I need a break. It might be a good time to just go through the motions until I get to the other side. I don't want to think about food or diabesity.

There Is no great raw healing going on, nothing exciting. I'm not learning anything new. Instead I'm getting better at what I know. It's so boring. I stepped out of the boat, but I didn't get thin. I learned to deal with my problems. The way I feel right now is powerful, but I was hoping to get skinny.

Ghost Bone

My tooth, my bad tooth, cracked in half at the root. Now I'm going through a process to get an implant. This is affecting my eating. I'm in some pain and I'm constipated. This is making everything harder.

After my tooth was removed I was given a bone graft. Now I feel like I've got a ghost living in my jaw. True or not, my lupus doesn't like it. One more problem to work through.

As I go through my day to day life more things come up that harm my effort to bring better health into my life.

So What's THE Answer?

THE answer is there is no answer, there are many and none. Individuals vary, and some of us have many problems that lead to obesity.

My answers are my own. I'm glad for them, and maybe they will work for others, but maybe not. There is no right way. There are many roads to Rome.

I suppose the best answer is to just keep swimming. Keep your eyes open, think about what has worked, and what makes sense. Never give up and take what you may receive.

Be grateful. Keep going. Rest when you need to. Right now is all you really have. I don't have anything new to say. It's what we all thought because bodies know.

For me, the answer is to keep the voices in my head from screaming at me, to keep from eating to the point of discomfort, and to enjoy life.

The best answer, the one that makes the most sense, is to do what generates health. That's a bitter pill. If only good health centered around eating ice cream and being very thin. Then I'd be on the right track.

How to Lose Weight

Cancer will take it off of you. Getting sick will use up one's reserves of fat. No matter how much you eat, if you don't make insulin you will lose weight. One time a big lupus flare up cut 10 pounds off me in less than a week.

Being in control can work. At least for a while. Exercise can work for some, not for all, unless it's an excessive amount. I've done lots of programs and followed advice. Some things I've taken with me, most of it I left by the wayside. The way of weight loss is an elusive little unicorn. I think the real trick is in that stomach. Getting comfortable with certain feelings. Once I can decide I like to feel a certain way then it's just a matter of following the signs.

The body makes the path.

I'm not sure if I'm ever going to lose weight again. As I write this I'm crying. It's been a few years since I've cried. What I'm letting go of, why it's so sad, don't know. I'm so tired of trying to bulldoze the Sahara instead of just sailing down the Coast.

If I let it just be, I know that my weight will end up being what it should. That means taking care of my health, physical and mental, to the best of my ability, and letting God do the rest. Sometimes the power is in accepting and fighting against the things that can be changed. I'm not made to be small. I will never be beautiful. This doesn't mean I can't have a beautiful life.

What Happened With My Weight

It's complicated. Basically, It just does what it does. Other than monitoring it I do nothing else about it. It's like my height. Eating has been an on and off sort of thing. Now I know hunger is a clue to health, not a character flaw. I pay attention, I buy foods that don't trick my system, and I take care of myself. Controlling size is an illusion. It only lasts so long, and usually backfires. Whatever size I am is what I need to be. I don't have to like it. Accepting this and making peace with it brings me closer to being happy. No one can ask for more.

As hard as I try not to care about my weight, I still care. I suppose I always will. Instead of trying to not see the white bear, I'm just trying to think about it less and think about other things.

Weight is, after all, just a number in time. Right now I am living in a body, and that is a great gift. This gift is beyond measure. It may not be the most beautiful body, the one I wanted, or even one I like, but this is something to be revered and respected. Life is so special and nothing to be taken for granted. I don't have to love myself to respect the wondrous task I have been assigned. Life in a body is hard but life in a body is glorious, no matter the body. That is what is important, not the size of the body.

Who Do I Want To Be?

I'm not certain what I want to do with myself. The future is open and I'm excited for it. While I know who I want in it, I don't know where I want to be or who I want to be.

If I could fly I would, I'd like to be kind, smart, funny, witty, loved, never wrong, and creative. The dramatic side of me would like to be admired. The calm side would like to live alone by the sea. What exactly this person looks like and acts like I just don't know.

My whole life, at least since I was five, what I really wanted to be was thin. That was what I wanted the most. Above healthy, above happy, above pretty, and even above comfortable, being skinny, or at least not fat was my greatest aspiration. That seems so stupid now. So what does that leave me with? A big hole in my being of daily thoughts needs to be filled. Just what do I put there? Why do I have this emptiness? The blank space is so uncomfortable. Like being in a room with someone in silence.

I don't feel alone when I am with myself anymore.

I think what I really want to be is happy.

When I was small my brother named me tink. That was his charming way of saying stinky. That's who I want to be. Stinky. There is a picture, a few of them. They are black and white and some have my brother in them. The two of us are in the yard and on the swing set. There the two of us sat on the swings, Mike and Tink. Nothing was ever as close to the truth as this.

I am Stinky and I'm living my life in this body, no matter what size.

-Not Really Done Yet-

-Opinions Subject to Change-

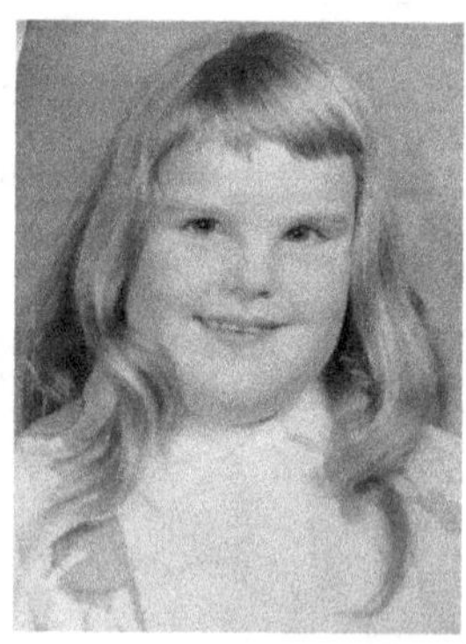

Love, Tink (Stinky)